QUICK AND EASY
CHINESE
STIR-FRIES

T009796

QUICK AND EASY
CHINESE
STIR-FRIES

60 FAST, HEALTHY RECIPES FULL OF SPICE AND TASTE,
SHOWN STEP BY STEP WITH 300 PHOTOGRAPHS

LINDA DOESER

southwater

This edition is published by Southwater, an imprint of Anness Publishing Ltd, Hermes House,
88–89 Blackfriars Road, London SE1 8HA; tel. 020 7401 2077; fax 020 7633 9499

www.southwaterbooks.com; www.annesspublishing.com

If you like the images in this book and would like to investigate using them for publishing, promotions
or advertising, please visit our website www.practicalpictures.com for more information.

UK agent: The Manning Partnership Ltd; tel. 01225 478444; fax 01225 478440; sales@manning-partnership.co.uk
UK distributor: Grantham Book Services Ltd; tel. 01476 541080; fax 01476 541061; orders@gbs.tbs-ltd.co.uk
North American agent/distributor: National Book Network; tel. 301 459 3366; fax 301 429 5746; www.nbnbooks.com
Australian agent/distributor: Pan Macmillan Australia; tel. 1300 135 113; fax 1300 135 103; customer.service@macmillan.com.au
New Zealand agent/distributor: David Bateman Ltd; tel. (09) 415 7664; fax (09) 415 8892

Publisher: Joanna Lorenz
Project Editor: Linda Doeser
Copy Editor: Harriette Lanzer
Designers: Ian Sandom, Siân Keogh
Photography: Karl Adamson, Edward Allwright, David Armstrong, Steve Baxter, James Duncan,
Michelle Garrett, Amanda Heywood, Patrick McLeavey, Michael Michaels, Thomas Odulate
Styling: Madeleine Brehaut, Michelle Garrett, Maria Kelly, Blake Minton, Kirsty Rawlings
Food for Photography: Carla Capalbo, Kit Chan, Elizabeth Wolf-Cohen, Joanne Craig, Nicola Fowler, Carole Handslip,
Jane Hartshorn, Shehzad Husain, Wendy Lee, Lucy McKelvie, Annie Nichols, Jane Stevenson, Steven Wheeler
Illustrations: Madeleine David

ETHICAL TRADING POLICY

Because of our ongoing ecological investment programme, you, as our customer, can have the pleasure and reassurance of knowing
that a tree is being cultivated on your behalf to naturally replace the materials used to make the book you are holding.
For further information about this scheme, go to www.annesspublishing.com/trees

© Anness Publishing Limited 1998, 2009

All rights reserved. No part of this publication may be reproduced, stored in a retrieval system, or transmitted in any way or by any means,
electronic, mechanical, photocopying, recording or otherwise, without the prior written permission of the copyright holder.

A CIP catalogue record for this book is available from the British Library.

NOTES

For all recipes, quantities are given in both metric and imperial measures and, where appropriate, in standard cups and spoons.
Follow one set of measures, but not a mixture, because they are not interchangeable.
Standard spoon and cup measures are level. 1 tsp = 5ml, 1 tbsp = 15ml, 1 cup = 250ml/8fl oz.
Australian standard tablespoons are 20ml. Australian readers should use 3 tsp in place
of 1 tbsp for measuring small quantities.
American pints are 16fl oz/2 cups. American readers should use 20fl oz/2.5 cups in place
of 1 pint when measuring liquids.
Electric oven temperatures in this book are for conventional ovens. When using a fan oven, the temperature will probably need to be
reduced by about 10–20°C/20–40°F. Since ovens vary, you should check with your manufacturer's instruction book for guidance.
Medium (US large) eggs are used unless otherwise stated.

Main front cover image shows Lemon Grass Pork – for recipe, see page 46

Previously published as *Quick and Easy Chinese Kitchen*

PUBLISHER'S NOTE

Although the advice and information in this book are believed to be accurate and true at the time of going to press, neither the
authors nor the publisher can accept any legal responsibility or liability for any errors or omissions that may be made nor for
any inaccuracies nor for any harm or injury that comes about from following instructions or advice in this book.

CONTENTS

INTRODUCTION

Chinese food has become increasingly popular in the West during the last three decades, moving gradually from restaurants to home kitchens. Part of its charm, for the cook at least, is the speed at which it can be prepared. Delicious, aromatic and unusual meals can be ready in minutes. Moreover, because the food is cooked so rapidly it keeps many of its vitamins, its colour and texture.

∾

The wok and stir-frying reign supreme in the Chinese kitchen. This round-based pan is designed to cook finely sliced or chopped ingredients rapidly and evenly. The food must be kept on the move throughout cooking, but it takes only a little practice to perfect the technique. But Chinese cooking is not all stir-frying – steaming, poaching, deep-frying and baking all play important roles, too.

∾

This book begins with a useful glossary of some more unfamiliar ingredients, spices and sauces. This is followed by advice on equipment and a basic guide to stir-frying, deep-frying and steaming in a wok. The recipes are divided into six chapters: Soups & Appetizers, Fish & Seafood, Meat & Poultry, Vegetables, Noodles & Rice, and Desserts. All the recipes are superbly illustrated in colour with easy-to-follow step-by-step instructions. Hints and tips throughout offer helpful suggestions and variations of the recipes.

∾

From Corn and Crab Meat Soup to Toffee Apples, all the dishes can be cooked in 15 minutes and many of them take even less time.

INGREDIENTS

Bamboo shoots Mild-flavoured, tender shoots of the young bamboo, widely available fresh, or sliced or halved in cans.

Basil Several different types of basil are used in Asian cooking. Thai cooks use two varieties, holy and sweet basil, but ordinary basil works well.

Bean curd See under Tofu.

Beansprouts Shoots of the mung bean, usually available from supermarkets. They add a crisp texture to stir-fries.

Black bean sauce Made of salted black beans crushed and mixed with flour and spices (such as ginger, garlic or chilli) to form a thickish paste. It is sold in jars or cans and, once opened, should be kept in the refrigerator.

Cardamom pods Available both as small green pods and larger black pods containing seeds, they have a strong aromatic quality.

Cashew nuts Whole cashew nuts feature prominently in Chinese stir-fries, especially those with chicken.

Cassia bark A form of cinnamon, but with a more robust flavour.

Chilli bean sauce Made from fermented bean paste mixed with hot chilli and other seasonings. Sold in jars, some chilli bean sauces are quite mild, but some are very hot. You will have to try out the various brands yourself to see which one is to your taste.

Chilli oil Made from dried red chillies, garlic, onions, salt and vegetable oil, this is used more as a dip than as a cooking ingredient.

Chilli sauce A very hot sauce made from chillies, vinegar, sugar and salt. Usually sold in bottles, it should be used sparingly in cooking or as a dip. Tabasco sauce can be a substitute.

Chillies There is a wide range of fresh and dried chillies from which to choose. Generally the larger the chilli, the milder the flavour, but there are some exceptions, and the only way to gauge potency is by taste. Remove the seeds for a milder flavour. Whether using dried or fresh chillies, take care when preparing them as their seeds and flesh can "burn": wash your hands immediately afterwards or, better still, wear rubber gloves – and never rub your eyes.

Chinese cabbage Also known as Chinese leaves, two sorts are widely available. The most commonly seen variety has a pale green colour and tightly wrapped elongated head, and about two-thirds of the cabbage is stem which has a crunchy texture. The other type has a shorter and fatter head with curlier, pale yellow or green leaves, and white stems.

Chinese chives Better known as garlic chives, these are sometimes sold with their flowers.

Chinese five-spice powder This flavouring contains star anise, pepper, fennel, cloves and cinnamon.

Chinese pancakes Thin flour and water pancakes with no added seasonings or spices. They are available fresh or frozen.

Chinese rice wine Made from glutinous rice, this is also known as yellow wine – *huang jin* or *chiew* – because of its colour. The best variety is called Shao Hsing or Shaoxing and comes from the south-east of China. Dry sherry may be used as a substitute.

Coconut milk and cream Coconut milk should not be confused with the "milk" or juice found inside a fresh coconut (though the latter makes a refreshing drink). The coconut milk used for cooking is produced from the white flesh of the nut. If left to stand, the thick part of the milk will rise to the surface like cream.

To make your own, break open a fresh coconut and remove the brown inner skin from the flesh. Grate sufficient flesh to measure 400ml/14 fl oz/1⅔ cups. Place the grated flesh, together with 300ml/½ pint/1¼ cups water, in a blender or food processor fitted with a metal blade and process for 1 minute. Strain the mixture through a sieve lined with muslin into a bowl. Gather up the corners of the muslin and squeeze out the liquid. The coconut milk is then ready to use, but you should stir it before use.

Coconut milk is also available in cans, as a soluble powder and as creamed coconut which is sold in block form. Powder and creamed coconut make a poor milk, but are useful for sauces and dressings.

Coriander Fresh coriander has a strong, pungent smell that combines well with other rich flavours. The white coriander root is used when the green colouring is not required. The seeds are also used, whole and ground.

Cornflour paste To make cornflour paste, mix 4 parts cornflour with about 5 parts cold water until smooth.

Cumin Available as whole seeds and as a powder, cumin has a strong, slightly bitter flavour and is used mainly in Indian recipes, and also in many Asian dishes.

Curry paste Curry paste is traditionally made by pounding fresh herbs and spices in a mortar with a pestle. The two types of Thai curry paste, red and green, are made with red and green chillies respectively. Other ingredients vary with individual cooks, but red curry paste typically contains ginger, shallots, garlic, coriander and cumin seeds and lime juice, as well as chillies. Herbs and flavourings in green curry paste usually include spring onions, fresh coriander, kaffir lime leaves, ginger, garlic and lemon grass. Making curry paste is time-consuming, but it tastes excellent and keeps well. Ready-made pastes, available in packets and tubs, are satisfactory substitutes.

Top shelf, left to right: *garlic, ginger, lemon grass, dried shrimps, Thai fish sauce, Szechuan peppercorns, sweet chilli sauce, ground coriander, galangal, Chinese five-spice powder, fresh green chillies*

Middle shelf: *dried red chillies, peanuts (skins on), cardamom pods, cashew nuts (in jar), peanuts (skins off), kaffir lime leaves, tamarind, hoisin sauce, salted black beans, chilli oil*

Bottom shelf, back row: *sake, rice vinegar, Chinese rice wine*

Bottom shelf, middle row: *sesame oil, mirin, peanut oil, fresh coriander, cumin seeds*

Bottom shelf, front row: *basil, dried shrimp paste, red and green chillies, flaked coconut and creamed coconut, light soy sauce, oyster sauce, pieces of coconut, whole coconut*

Lemon grass Also known as citronella, lemon grass has a long, pale green stalk and a bulbous end similar to that of a spring onion. Only the bottom 13cm/5in are used. It has a woody texture and an aromatic, lemony scent. Unless finely chopped, it is always removed before serving because it is so fibrous.

Dashi Light Japanese stock, available in powder form. The flavour derives from kelp seaweed. Diluted vegetable stock made from a cube may be substituted.

Dried shrimps and shrimp paste Dried shrimps are tiny shrimps that are salted and dried. They are used as a seasoning for stir-fried dishes. Soak them first in warm water until soft, then either process them in a blender or food processor or pound them in a mortar with a pestle. Shrimp paste, also known as *terasi*, is a dark, odorous paste made from fermented shrimps. Use sparingly.

Fish sauce The most commonly used flavouring in Thai food. Fish sauce (*nam pla*) is used in Thai cooking in the same way as soy sauce is used in Chinese dishes. It is made from salted anchovies and has a strong, salty flavour.

Galangal Fresh galangal, also known as *lengkuas*, tastes and looks a little like

ginger with a pinkish tinge to its skin. Prepare it in the same way. It is also available dried and ground.

Garlic Garlic, together with ginger, is an indispensable ingredient in Chinese and Asian cooking.

Ginger Fresh ginger root has a sharp, distinctive flavour. Choose firm, plump pieces of fresh root with unwrinkled, shiny skins.

Gram flour Made from ground chick-peas, this flour has a unique flavour and is worth seeking out in Indian food stores.

Hoisin sauce A thick, dark brownish-red sauce which is sweet and spicy.

Kaffir lime leaves These are used rather like bay leaves, but to give an aromatic lime flavour to dishes. The fresh leaves are available from oriental food stores and can be frozen for future use.

Lengkuas See under Galangal.

Mirin A mild, sweet, Japanese rice wine used in cooking.

Miso A fermented bean paste that adds richness and flavour to Japanese soups.

Mooli A member of the radish family with a fresh, slightly peppery taste and white skin and flesh. Unlike other radishes, it is good when cooked, but should be salted and allowed to drain first, as it has a high water content. It is widely used in Chinese cooking and may be carved into an elaborate garnish.

Mushrooms Chinese shiitake mushrooms are used both fresh and dried to add texture and flavour to a dish. Wood ears are used in their dried form. All dried mushrooms need to be soaked in warm water for 20–30 minutes before use. Dried mushrooms are expensive, but a small quantity goes a long way.

Noodles: Cellophane noodles, also known as bean thread, transparent or glass noodles, are made from ground mung beans. Dried noodles must be soaked in hot water before cooking.

Egg noodles are made from wheat flour, egg and water. The dough is flattened and then shredded or extruded through a pasta machine to the required shape and thickness.

Rice noodles are made from ground rice and water. They range in thickness from very thin to wide ribbons and sheets. Dried ribbon rice noodles are usually sold tied together in bundles. Fresh rice noodles are also available. Rinse rice noodles in warm water and drain before use.

Rice vermicelli are thin, brittle noodles that look like white hair and are sold in large bundles. They cook almost instantly in hot liquid, provided the noodles are first soaked in warm water. They can also be deep-fried.

Somen noodles are delicate, thin, white Japanese noodles made from wheat flour in dried form, usually tied in bundles held together with a paper band.

Udon noodles, also Japanese, are made of wheat flour and water. They are usually round, but can also be flat and are available fresh, precooked or dried.

Nori Paper-thin sheets of Japanese seaweed.

Oyster sauce Made from oyster extract, this is used in many Asian fish dishes, soups and sauces.

Pak choi Also known as bok choi, this is a leaf vegetable with long, smooth, milky white stems and dark green foliage.

Palm sugar Strongly flavoured, hard brown sugar made from the sap of the coconut

palm tree. It is available in oriental stores. If you have trouble finding it, use soft dark brown sugar instead.

Peanut oil This oil can be heated to a high temperature, making it perfect for stir-frying and deep-frying.

Peanuts Used in wok cookery to add flavour and a crunchy texture. The thin red skins must be removed before cooking, by immersing the peanuts in boiling water for a few minutes and then rubbing off the skins.

Red bean paste A reddish-brown paste made from puréed red beans and crystallized sugar. It is sold in cans.

Rice Long-grain rice is generally used for savoury dishes. There are many high-quality varieties, coming from a range of countries. Basmati, which means fragrant in Hindi, is generally acknowledged as the king of rices. Thai jasmine rice is also fragrant and slightly sticky.

Rice vinegar There are two basic types of rice vinegar: red vinegar is made from fermented rice and has a distinctive dark colour and depth of flavour; white vinegar is stronger in flavour as it is distilled from rice. If rice vinegar is unavailable, cider vinegar may be substituted.

Sake A strong, powerful, fortified rice wine from Japan.

Dried noodles
1 ribbon noodles, 2 somen noodles,
3 udon noodles, 4 soba noodles,
5 egg ribbon noodles, 6 medium egg noodles,
7 cellophane noodles, 8 rice sheets,
9 rice vermicelli, 10 egg noodles,
11 rice ribbon noodles

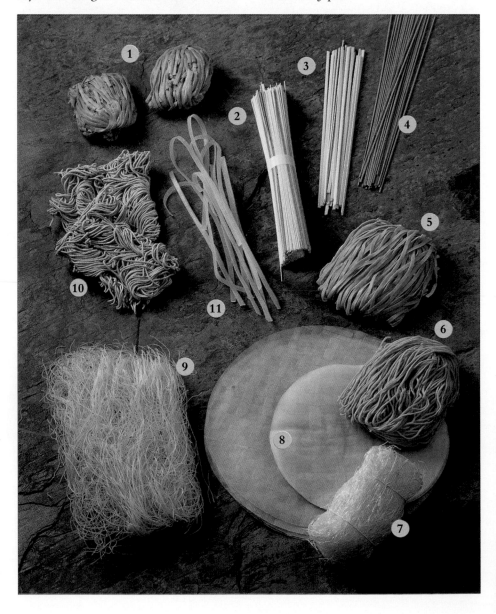

Sesame oil This is used more for flavouring than for cooking. It is very intensely flavoured, so only a little is required.

Soy sauce A major seasoning ingredient in Asian cooking, this is made from fermented soy beans combined with yeast, salt and sugar. Chinese soy sauce falls into two main categories: light and dark. Light soy sauce has more flavour than the sweeter dark soy sauce, which gives food a rich, reddish colour.

Spring roll wrappers Paper-thin wrappers made from wheat or rice flour and water. Wheat wrappers are usually sold frozen and should be thawed and separated before use. Rice flour wrappers are dry and must be soaked before use.

Sweet potato The sweet richness of this red tuber marries well with the hot-and-sour flavours of South-east Asia. In Japan the sweet potato is used to make delicious candies and sweetmeats.

Szechuan peppercorns Also known as *farchiew*, these aromatic red peppercorns are best used roasted and ground. They are not so hot as either white or black peppercorns, but do add a unique taste.

Tamarind The brown, sticky pulp of the bean-like seed pod of the tamarind tree. It is used in Thai and Indonesian cooking to add tartness to recipes, rather as western cooks use vinegar or lemon juice. It is usually sold dried or pulped. The pulp is diluted with water and strained before use. Soak 25g/1oz tamarind pulp in 150ml/¼ pint/⅔ cup warm water for about 10 minutes. Squeeze out as much tamarind juice as possible by pressing all the liquid through a sieve.

Terasi See under Dried Shrimps and Shrimp Paste.

Tofu This custard-like preparation of puréed and pressed soya beans, also known as bean curd, is high in protein. Plain tofu is bland in flavour but readily absorbs the flavours of the food with which it is cooked. Tofu is also available

smoked and marinated. Firm blocks of tofu are best suited to stir-frying.

Turmeric A member of the ginger family, turmeric is a rich, golden-coloured root. If you are using the fresh root, wear rubber gloves when peeling it to avoid staining your skin. Turmeric is also available in powder form.

Wasabi This is an edible root, which is used in Japanese cooking to make a condiment with a sharp, pungent and fiery flavour. It is very similar to horseradish and is available fresh, and in powder and paste form.

Water chestnuts Walnut-sized bulbs from an Asian water plant that look like sweet chestnuts. They are sold fresh by some oriental food stores, but are more readily available canned.

Wonton wrappers Small, paper-thin squares of wheat flour and egg dough.

Top shelf, left to right: *fresh egg noodles, wonton wrappers, water chestnuts, cellophane noodles, gram flour, spring roll wrappers*
Middle shelf: *dried Chinese mushrooms, pak choi, tofu, dried egg noodles, Chinese pancakes*
Bottom shelf, at back: *rice; (in basket) mangetouts, baby sweetcorn, shallots, shiitake mushrooms; Chinese cabbage, rice vermicelli*
Bottom shelf, at front: *bamboo shoots, beansprouts, wood ears (mushrooms), spring onions, yard-long beans*

Yard-long beans Long, thin beans similar to French beans but three or four times longer. Cut into smaller lengths and use just like ordinary green beans.

Yellow bean sauce A thick paste made from salted, fermented yellow soya beans, crushed with flour and sugar.

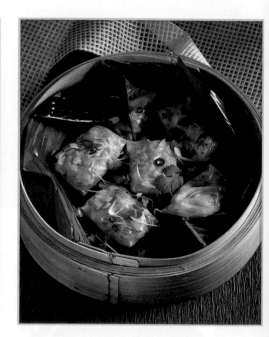

SOUPS &
APPETIZERS

Chinese Tofu and Lettuce Soup

This light, clear soup is brimful of nourishing, tasty vegetables.

INGREDIENTS

Serves 4

30ml/2 tbsp groundnut or
  sunflower oil
200g/7oz smoked or marinated
  tofu, cubed
3 spring onions, sliced diagonally
2 garlic cloves, cut in thin strips
1 carrot, thinly sliced in rounds
1 litre/1¾ pints/4 cups vegetable stock
30ml/2 tbsp soy sauce
15ml/1 tbsp dry sherry or vermouth
5ml/1 tsp sugar
115g/4oz Cos lettuce, shredded
salt and ground black pepper

1 Heat the oil in a preheated wok, then stir-fry the tofu cubes until browned. Drain and set aside on kitchen paper.

2 Add the onions, garlic and carrot to the wok and stir-fry for 2 minutes. Pour in the stock, soy sauce, dry sherry or vermouth, sugar and lettuce. Heat through gently for 1 minute, season to taste and serve hot.

Crab and Egg Noodle Broth

This delicious broth is the ideal solution when you are hungry, time is short and you need a fast, nutritious and filling meal.

INGREDIENTS

Serves 4

75g/3oz thin egg noodles
25g/1oz/2 tbsp unsalted butter
1 small bunch spring onions, chopped
1 celery stick, sliced
1 medium carrot, cut into batons
1.2 litres/2 pints/5 cups chicken stock
60ml/4 tbsp dry sherry
115g/4oz white crab meat, fresh or frozen
pinch of celery salt
pinch of cayenne pepper
10ml/2 tsp lemon juice
1 small bunch coriander or flat-leaf parsley, roughly chopped, to garnish

1 Bring a large saucepan of salted water to the boil. Toss in the egg noodles and cook according to the instructions on the packet. Cool under cold running water and leave immersed in water until required.

COOK'S TIP

Fresh and frozen crab meat have a better flavour than canned crab, which tends to taste rather bland.

2 Heat the butter in another large pan, add the spring onions, celery and carrot, cover and cook the vegetables over a gentle heat for 3-4 minutes until soft.

3 Add the chicken stock and dry sherry, bring to the boil and simmer for a further 5 minutes.

4 Flake the crab meat between your fingers on to a plate and remove any stray pieces of shell.

5 Drain the noodles and add to the broth together with the crab meat. Season to taste with celery salt and cayenne pepper and stir in the lemon juice. Return to a simmer.

6 Ladle the broth into shallow soup plates, scatter with roughly chopped coriander or parsley and serve immediately.

Corn and Crab Meat Soup

Surprisingly, this soup originated in the United States, but it has since been introduced into mainstream Chinese cookery. It is important that you make sure you use creamed sweetcorn in the recipe to achieve exactly the right consistency.

INGREDIENTS

Serves 4

115g/4oz crab meat or chicken
   breast fillet
2.5ml/$\frac{1}{2}$ tsp finely chopped root
   ginger
2 egg whites
30ml/2 tbsp milk
15ml/1 tbsp cornflour paste
600ml/1 pint/2$\frac{1}{2}$ cups stock
225g/8oz can creamed sweetcorn
salt and ground black pepper
finely chopped spring onions,
   to garnish

1 Flake the crab meat roughly with chopsticks or chop the chicken breast. Mix the crab meat or chicken with the chopped root ginger.

2 Beat the egg whites until frothy, add the milk and cornflour paste and beat again until smooth. Blend with the crab meat or chicken breast.

3 Bring the stock to the boil in a wok. Add the creamed sweetcorn and bring back to the boil once more.

4 Stir in the crab meat or chicken breast and egg-white mixture, adjust the seasoning and simmer gently until cooked. Serve garnished with finely chopped spring onions.

Chicken and Asparagus Soup

This is a very delicate and delicious soup, with chicken and asparagus simply and quickly prepared in a wok.

INGREDIENTS

Serves 4
150g/5oz chicken breast fillet
5ml/1 tsp egg white
5ml/1 tsp cornflour paste
115g/4oz fresh or canned asparagus
750ml/1¼ pints/3 cups stock
salt and ground black pepper
fresh coriander leaves, to garnish

1 Cut the chicken meat into thin slices, each about the size of a postage stamp. Mix with a pinch of salt, then add the egg white and finally the cornflour paste.

2 Discard the tough stems of the asparagus, and cut the tender spears diagonally into short lengths.

3 Bring the stock to a rolling boil in a wok. Add the asparagus, bring back to the boil and cook for 2 minutes. (This is not necessary if you are using canned asparagus.)

4 Add the chicken, stir to separate and bring back to the boil once more. Adjust the seasoning to taste. Serve hot, garnished with fresh coriander leaves.

Crispy "Seaweed"

Surprisingly, the very popular and rather exotic-sounding "seaweed" served in Chinese restaurants is, in fact, just ordinary spring greens.

INGREDIENTS

Serves 4
450g/1lb spring greens
vegetable oil, for deep frying
2.5ml/¹/₂ tsp salt
5ml/1 tsp caster sugar
15ml/1 tbsp ground fried fish, to garnish (optional)

1 Cut off the hard stalks in the centre of each spring green leaf. Pile the leaves on top of each other, and roll into a tight sausage shape. Thinly cut the leaves into fine shreds. Spread them out to dry.

2 Heat the oil in a wok until hot. Deep fry the shredded greens in batches, stirring to separate them.

3 Remove the greens with a slotted spoon as soon as they are crispy, but before they turn brown. Drain. Sprinkle the salt and sugar evenly all over the "seaweed", mix well, garnish with ground fish, if liked, and serve.

Sesame Seed Prawn Toasts

Use uncooked prawns for this dish, as ready-cooked ones will tend to separate from the bread during cooking.

INGREDIENTS

Serves 4
225g/8oz uncooked prawns, peeled
25g/1oz lard
1 egg white, lightly beaten
5ml/1 tsp finely chopped spring onions
2.5ml/¹/₂ tsp finely chopped root ginger
15ml/1 tbsp Chinese rice wine or dry sherry
15ml/1 tbsp cornflour paste
115–150g/4–5oz white sesame seeds
6 large slices white bread
vegetable oil, for deep frying
salt and ground black pepper

1 Chop together the prawns with the lard to form a smooth paste. In a bowl, mix with all the other ingredients except the sesame seeds and bread.

2 Spread the sesame seeds evenly on a large plate or tray; spread the prawn paste thickly on one side of each slice of bread, then press, spread side down, on to the seeds.

3 Heat the oil in a wok until medium-hot; fry 2–3 slices of the sesame bread at a time, spread side down, for 2–3 minutes. Remove and drain. Cut each slice into six or eight fingers (without crusts).

Braised Fish Fillet with Mushrooms

This is the Chinese stir-fried version of the French *filets de sole bonne femme* (sole cooked with mushrooms and wine sauce).

INGREDIENTS

Serves 4
450g/1lb lemon sole or plaice fillets
5ml/1 tsp salt
1/2 egg white
30ml/2 tbsp cornflour paste
about 600ml/1 pint/2 1/2 cups
  vegetable oil
15ml/1 tbsp finely chopped
  spring onions
2.5ml/1/2 tsp finely chopped fresh
  root ginger
115g/4oz white mushrooms,
  thinly sliced
5ml/1 tsp light brown sugar
15ml/1 tbsp light soy sauce
30ml/2 tbsp Chinese rice wine or
  dry sherry
15ml/1 tbsp brandy
about 120ml/4fl oz/1/2 cup stock
few drops sesame oil

1 Trim off the soft bones along the edge of the fish, but leave the skin on. Cut each fillet into bite-sized pieces. Mix the fish with a little salt, the egg white and about half of the cornflour paste.

2 Heat the oil in a preheated wok until medium-hot, add the fish, slice by slice, and stir gently so the pieces do not stick. Remove after about 1 minute and drain. Pour off the excess oil, leaving about 30ml/2 tbsp in the wok.

3 Stir-fry the spring onions, ginger and mushrooms for 1 minute. Add the sugar, soy sauce, rice wine or sherry, brandy and stock. Bring to the boil. Return the fish to the wok and braise for 1 minute. Stir in the remaining cornflour paste to thicken the sauce and sprinkle with sesame oil.

— COOK'S TIP —

You could substitute straw mushrooms, so called because they are grown on beds of rice straw. They have a subtle flavour and a slightly slippery texture.

Prawn Fu-yung

This is a very colourful dish that is simple to make in a wok. Most of the preparation can be done well in advance.

INGREDIENTS

Serves 4
3 eggs, beaten, reserving 5ml/1 tsp
  egg white
15ml/1 tbsp finely chopped
  spring onions
45–60ml/3–4 tbsp vegetable oil
225g/8oz uncooked prawns, peeled
10ml/2 tsp cornflour paste
175g/6oz green peas
15ml/1 tbsp Chinese rice wine or
  dry sherry
salt

1 Beat the eggs with a pinch of the salt and a few pieces of the spring onions. Heat a little oil in a preheated wok over a moderate heat. Add the egg mixture and stir to scramble. Remove the scrambled eggs and reserve.

2 Mix the prawns with a little salt, 5ml/1 tsp egg white and the cornflour paste. Stir-fry the peas in hot oil for 30 seconds Add the prawns.

3 Add the spring onions. Stir-fry for 1 minute, then stir the mixture into the scrambled egg with a little salt and the wine or sherry and serve.

Chilli Prawns

This delightful, spicy combination makes a lovely, light main course for a casual supper. Serve with rice, noodles or even freshly cooked pasta and a leafy green salad.

INGREDIENTS

Serves 3–4
45ml/3 tbsp olive oil
2 shallots, chopped
2 garlic cloves, chopped
1 fresh red chilli, chopped
450g/1lb ripe tomatoes, skinned, seeded and chopped
15ml/1 tbsp tomato purée
1 bay leaf
1 thyme sprig
90ml/6 tbsp dry white wine
450g/1lb cooked large prawns, peeled
salt and ground black pepper
roughly torn basil leaves, to garnish

1 Heat the oil in a pan, then add the shallots, garlic and chilli and fry until the garlic starts to brown.

2 Add the tomatoes, tomato purée, bay leaf, thyme, wine and seasoning. Bring to the boil, then reduce the heat and cook gently for about 10 minutes, stirring occasionally, until the sauce has thickened. Discard the herbs.

3 Stir the prawns into the sauce and heat through for a few minutes. Taste and adjust the seasoning. Scatter over the basil leaves and serve at once.

COOK'S TIP

For a milder flavour, remove all the seeds from the chilli.

Scallops with Ginger

Scallops are at their best in the winter, but are available frozen throughout the year. Rich and creamy, this dish is very simple to make and utterly scrumptious.

INGREDIENTS

Serves 4
8–12 scallops, shelled
40g/1½oz/3 tbsp butter
2.5cm/1in fresh root ginger, finely chopped
1 bunch spring onions, sliced diagonally
60ml/4 tbsp white vermouth
250ml/8fl oz/1 cup crème fraîche
salt and ground black pepper
chopped fresh parsley, to garnish

1 Remove the tough muscle opposite the coral on each scallop. Separate the coral and cut the white part of the scallop in half horizontally.

2 Melt the butter in a frying pan. Add the scallops, including the corals, and sauté for about 2 minutes until lightly browned. Take care not to overcook the scallops as this will make them tough.

3 Lift out the scallops with a slotted spoon and transfer to a warmed serving dish. Keep warm.

4 Add the ginger and spring onions to the pan and stir-fry for 2 minutes. Pour in the vermouth and allow to bubble until it has almost evaporated. Stir in the crème fraîche and cook for a few minutes until the sauce has thickened. Taste and adjust the seasoning.

5 Pour the sauce over the scallops, sprinkle with parsley and serve immediately.

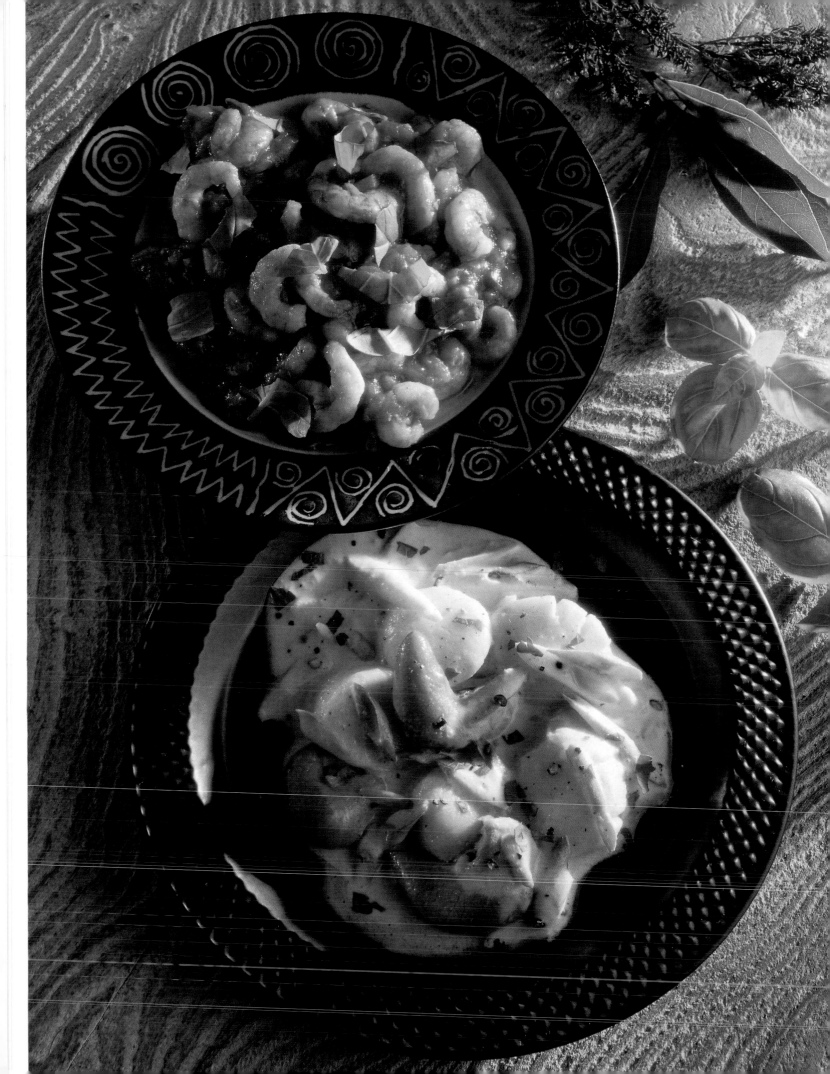

Stuffed Green Peppers

Stuffed peppers are given a different treatment here where they are deep fried in a wok and served with a tangy sauce.

INGREDIENTS

Serves 4
225–275g/8–10oz minced pork
4–6 water chestnuts, finely chopped
2 spring onions, finely chopped
2.5ml/¹⁄₂ tsp finely chopped fresh
  root ginger
15ml/1 tbsp light soy sauce
15ml/1 tbsp Chinese rice wine or
  dry sherry
3–4 green peppers, cored and seeded
15ml/1 tbsp cornflour
vegetable oil, for deep frying

For the sauce
10ml/2 tsp light soy sauce
5ml/1 tsp light brown sugar
1–2 fresh hot chillies, finely
  chopped (optional)
about 75ml/5 tbsp stock or water

1 Mix together the minced pork, water chestnuts, spring onions, ginger, soy sauce and rice wine or sherry in a bowl.

─────── COOK'S TIP ───────

You could substitute minced beef or lamb for the minced pork used in this recipe.

2 Cut the green peppers into halves or quarters. Stuff the sections with the pork mixture and sprinkle with a little cornflour.

3 Heat the oil in a preheated wok and deep fry the stuffed peppers, with the meat side down, for 2–3 minutes, then remove and drain.

4 Pour off the excess oil, then return the stuffed green peppers to the wok with the meat side up. Add the sauce ingredients, shaking the wok gently to make sure they do not stick to the bottom, and braise for 2–3 minutes. Carefully lift the stuffed peppers on to a serving dish, meat side up, and pour the sauce over them.

Stir-fried Beef and Broccoli

This spicy beef may be served with noodles or on a bed of boiled rice for a speedy and low-calorie Chinese meal.

INGREDIENTS

Serves 4
350g/12oz rump steak
15ml/1 tbsp cornflour
5ml/1 tsp sesame oil
350g/12oz broccoli, cut into small
   florets
4 spring onions, sliced diagonally
1 carrot, cut into matchstick strips
1 garlic clove, crushed
2.5cm/1in fresh root ginger, cut into
   very fine strips
120ml/4fl oz/½ cup beef stock
30ml/2 tbsp soy sauce
30ml/2 tbsp dry sherry
10ml/2 tsp soft light brown sugar
spring onion tassels, to garnish
   (optional)
noodles or rice, to serve

1 Trim the beef and cut into thin slices across the grain. Cut each slice into thin strips. Toss in the cornflour to coat thoroughly.

2 Heat the sesame oil in a preheated wok or large non-stick frying pan. Add the beef strips and stir-fry over a brisk heat for 3 minutes. Remove and set aside.

3 Add the broccoli, spring onions, carrot, garlic, ginger and stock to the wok or frying pan. Cover and simmer for 3 minutes. Uncover and cook, stirring, until all the stock has reduced entirely.

4 Mix the soy sauce, dry sherry and brown sugar together and add to the wok or frying pan with the beef. Cook for 2–3 minutes, stirring continuously. Spoon into a warmed serving dish and garnish with spring onion tassels, if liked. Serve on a bed of noodles or rice.

--- COOK'S TIP ---

To make spring onion tassels, trim the bulb base, then cut the green shoot so that the onion is 7.5cm/3in long. Shred to within 2.5cm/1in of the base and put into iced water for 1 hour.

Sizzling Beef with Celeriac Straw

The crisp celeriac matchsticks look like fine pieces of straw when stir-fried, and they have a mild celery-like flavour that is quite delicious.

Ingredients

Serves 4
450g/1lb celeriac
150ml/¼ pint/⅔ cup vegetable oil
1 red pepper
6 spring onions
450g/1lb rump steak
60ml/4 tbsp beef stock
30ml/2 tbsp sherry vinegar
10ml/2 tsp Worcestershire sauce
10ml/2 tsp tomato purée
salt and ground black pepper

1 Peel the celeriac and then cut into fine matchsticks, using a cleaver.

2 Heat a wok, then add two-thirds of the oil. When the oil is hot, fry the celeriac matchsticks in batches until golden brown and crispy. Drain well on kitchen paper.

3 Halve, core and seed the red pepper, then slice diagonally into 2.5cm/1in lengths. Slice the spring onions diagonally into 2.5cm/1in lengths.

4 Chop the beef into thin strips, across the grain of meat.

5 Heat the wok again and add the remaining oil. When the oil is hot, stir-fry the chopped red pepper and spring onion for 2–3 minutes.

6 Add the beef and stir-fry for 3–4 minutes more, until browned. Add the stock, vinegar, Worcestershire sauce and tomato purée. Season to taste and serve with the celeriac straw.

— Cook's Tip —

Avoid buying very large celeriac roots, as they tend to be woody or otherwise unpleasant in texture. As it is rather an unwieldy and knobbly vegetable, celeriac is easier to peel properly if you cut it into more or less even-sized slices first. Then peel each slice individually using a very sharp knife. They need to be peeled quite thickly to obtain a neat edge. You can then easily cut the slices into thin strips.

Spicy Chicken Stir-fry

The chicken is marinated in an aromatic blend of spices and stir-fried with crisp vegetables. If you find it too spicy, serve with a spoonful of soured cream or yogurt. It's delicious hot or cold.

INGREDIENTS

Serves 4

2.5ml/½ tsp ground turmeric
2.5ml/½ tsp ground ginger
5ml/1 tsp salt
5ml/1 tsp ground black pepper
10ml/2 tsp ground cumin
15ml/1 tbsp ground coriander
15ml/1 tbsp caster sugar
450g/1lb boneless chicken breasts, skinned
1 bunch spring onions
4 celery sticks
2 red peppers, seeded
1 yellow pepper, seeded
175g/6oz courgettes
175g/6oz mangetouts or sugar snap peas
sunflower oil, for frying
15ml/1 tbsp lime juice
15ml/1 tbsp clear honey

1 Mix together the turmeric, ginger, salt, pepper, cumin, coriander and sugar in a bowl until well combined.

2 Cut the chicken into bite-sized strips. Add to the spice mixture and stir to coat the chicken pieces thoroughly. Set aside.

3 Prepare the vegetables. Cut the spring onions, celery and peppers into 5cm/2in-long, thin strips. Cut the courgettes at a slight angle into thin rounds and top and tail the mangetouts or sugar snap peas.

4 Heat 30ml/2 tbsp of oil in a preheated wok or large frying pan. Stir-fry the chicken in batches until cooked through and golden brown, adding a little more oil if necessary. Remove from the pan and keep warm.

5 Add a little more oil to the pan and cook the spring onions, celery, peppers and courgettes over a medium heat for about 8–10 minutes, until beginning to soften and turn golden. Add the mangetouts or sugar snap peas and cook for a further 2 minutes.

6 Return the chicken to the pan, with the lime juice and honey. Cook for 2 minutes. Serve immediately.

Shredded Chicken with Celery

The tender chicken breast contrasts with the crunchy texture of the celery, and the red chillies add colour and flavour.

INGREDIENTS

Serves 4
275g/10oz boneless chicken breast, skinned
5ml/1 tsp salt
½ egg white, lightly beaten
10ml/2 tsp cornflour paste
475ml/16fl oz/2 cups vegetable oil
1 celery heart, thinly shredded
1–2 fresh red chillies, seeded and thinly shredded
1 spring onion, thinly shredded
few strips of fresh root ginger, thinly shredded
5ml/1 tsp light brown sugar
15ml/1 tbsp Chinese rice wine or dry sherry
few drops of sesame oil

1 Using a sharp knife, thinly shred the chicken. In a bowl, mix together a pinch of the salt, the egg white and cornflour paste. Stir in the chicken.

2 Heat the oil in a preheated wok, add the chicken and stir to separate the shreds. When the chicken turns white, remove with a strainer and drain. Keep warm.

3 Pour off all but 30ml/2 tbsp of the oil. Add the celery, chillies, spring onion and ginger to the wok and stir-fry for 1 minute. Add the chicken, remaining salt, sugar and rice wine or dry sherry. Cook for 1 minute, then add the sesame oil. Serve hot.

Chicken with Chinese Vegetables

This dish makes an excellent family main course served with rice or noodles, but also combines with a selection of other dishes to serve as part of a dinner party menu.

INGREDIENTS

Serves 4
225–275g/8–10oz boneless chicken, skinned
5ml/1 tsp salt
½ egg white, lightly beaten
10ml/2 tsp cornflour paste
60ml/4 tbsp vegetable oil
6–8 small dried shiitake mushrooms, soaked in hot water
115g/4oz canned sliced bamboo shoots, drained

115g/4oz mangetouts
1 spring onion, cut into short sections
few small pieces of fresh root ginger
5ml/1 tsp light brown sugar
15ml/1 tbsp light soy sauce
15ml/1 tbsp Chinese rice wine or dry sherry
few drops of sesame oil

1 Cut the chicken into thin slices, each about the size of an oblong postage stamp. Place it in a bowl and mix with a pinch of the salt, the egg white and the cornflour paste.

2 Heat the oil in a preheated wok, add the chicken and stir-fry over medium heat for about 30 seconds, then remove with a slotted spoon and keep warm.

3 Add the vegetables to the wok and stir-fry over high heat for about 1 minute. Add the remaining salt, the sugar and chicken. Blend, then add the soy sauce and rice wine or dry sherry. Stir for a further 1 minute. Sprinkle with the sesame oil and serve.

Stir-fried Turkey with Broccoli and Mushrooms

This is a really easy, tasty supper dish which works well with chicken too.

INGREDIENTS

Serves 4

115g/4oz broccoli florets
4 spring onions
5ml/1 tsp cornflour
45ml/3 tbsp oyster sauce
15ml/1 tbsp dark soy sauce
120ml/4fl oz/$\frac{1}{2}$ cup chicken stock
10ml/2 tsp lemon juice
45ml/3 tbsp groundnut oil
450g/1lb turkey steaks cut into strips, about 5mm x 5cm/$\frac{1}{4}$ x 2in
1 small onion, chopped
2 garlic cloves, crushed
10ml/2 tsp grated fresh root ginger
115g/4oz fresh shiitake mushrooms, sliced
75g/3oz baby sweetcorn, halved lengthways
15ml/1 tbsp sesame oil
salt and ground black pepper
egg noodles, to serve

1 Divide the broccoli florets into smaller sprigs and cut the stalks into thin diagonal slices.

2 Finely chop the white parts of the spring onions and slice the green parts into thin shreds.

3 In a bowl, blend together the cornflour, oyster sauce, soy sauce, stock and lemon juice. Set aside.

4 Heat 30ml/2 tbsp of the groundnut oil in a preheated wok. Add the turkey and stir-fry for 2 minutes until golden and crisp at the edges. Remove from the wok and keep warm.

5 Add the remaining groundnut oil to the wok and stir-fry the chopped onion, garlic and ginger over a medium heat for about 1 minute. Increase the heat to high, add the broccoli, mushrooms and sweetcorn and stir-fry for 2 minutes.

6 Return the turkey to the wok, then add the sauce with the chopped spring onion and seasoning. Cook, stirring, for about 1 minute until the sauce has thickened. Stir in the sesame oil. Serve immediately on a bed of egg noodles with the finely shredded spring onion scattered on top.

COOK'S TIP

Cook fresh egg noodles in salted boiling water, stirring occasionally to prevent them from sticking. They are ready within a few minutes. Follow the packet instructions for cooking dried egg noodles.

Black Bean and Vegetable Stir-fry

The secret of a quick stir-fry is proper preparation of all the ingredients first. It is important that the ingredients are added to the wok in the right order so that the larger or thicker pieces have a longer cooking time than the smaller pieces – even if this is a difference of only a few millimetres and a few seconds!

Ingredients

Serves 4
8 spring onions
225g/8oz button mushrooms
1 red pepper
1 green pepper
2 large carrots
60ml/4 tbsp sesame oil
2 garlic cloves, crushed
60ml/4 tbsp black bean sauce
90ml/6 tbsp warm water
225g/8oz beansprouts
salt and ground black pepper

1 Thinly slice the spring onions and button mushrooms.

2 Cut both the peppers in half, remove the seeds and slice the flesh into thin strips.

3 Cut the carrots in half. Cut each half into thin strips lengthways. Stack the slices and cut through them to make very fine strips.

4 Heat the oil in a large preheated wok until very hot. Add the spring onions and garlic and stir-fry for 30 seconds.

5 Add the mushrooms, peppers and carrots. Stir-fry for 5–6 minutes over a high heat until the vegetables are just beginning to soften.

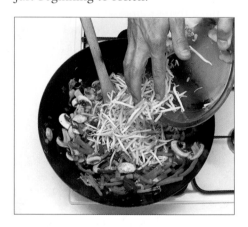

6 Mix the black bean sauce with the water. Add to the wok and cook for 3–4 minutes. Stir in the beansprouts and cook for 1 minute more, until all the vegetables are coated in the sauce. Season to taste, then serve at once.

COOK'S TIP

Black bean sauce is made from salted black beans – which have a very distinctive flavour – that have been crushed and mixed with a variety of spices, such as ginger and chilli. It is quite a thick paste and readily available in jars, bottles and cans from large supermarkets and oriental food stores. Store in the refrigerator after opening.

Soft Fried Noodles

This is a very basic dish for serving as an accompaniment or for those occasions when you are feeling a little peckish and fancy something simple. Break an egg into the noodles if you want to add protein. They are also good tossed with oyster sauce and a dollop of chilli black bean sauce.

INGREDIENTS

Serves 4-6
350g/12oz dried egg noodles
30ml/2 tbsp vegetable oil
30ml/2 tbsp finely chopped spring
  onions
soy sauce, to taste
salt and freshly ground black pepper

1 Cook the noodles in a large saucepan of boiling water until just tender, following the directions on the packet. Drain, rinse under cold running water and drain again thoroughly.

2 Heat the oil in a wok and swirl it around. Add the spring onions and fry for 30 seconds. Add the noodles, stirring gently to separate the strands.

3 Reduce the heat and fry the noodles until they are heated through, lightly browned and crisp on the outside, but still soft inside.

4 Season with soy sauce, salt and pepper. Serve at once.

Egg Fried Noodles

Yellow bean sauce gives these noodles a savoury flavour.

INGREDIENTS

Serves 4-6
350g/12oz medium-thick egg noodles
60ml/4 tbsp vegetable oil
4 spring onions, cut into 1cm/½in
  rounds
juice of 1 lime
15ml/1 tbsp soy sauce
2 garlic cloves, finely chopped
175g/6oz skinless, boneless chicken
  breast, sliced
175g/6oz raw prawns, peeled and
  deveined
175g/6oz squid, cleaned and cut into
  rings
15ml/1 tbsp yellow bean sauce
15ml/1 tbsp fish sauce
15ml/1 tbsp soft light brown sugar
2 eggs
coriander leaves, to garnish

1 Cook the noodles in a saucepan of boiling water until just tender, then drain well and set aside.

2 Heat half the oil in a wok or large frying pan. Add the spring onions, stir-fry for 2 minutes, then add the noodles, lime juice and soy sauce and stir-fry for 2-3 minutes. Transfer the mixture to a bowl and keep warm.

3 Heat the remaining oil in the wok or pan. Add the garlic, chicken, prawns and squid. Stir-fry over a high heat until cooked.

4 Stir in the yellow bean paste, fish sauce and sugar, then break the eggs into the mixture, stirring gently until they set.

5 Add the noodles, toss lightly to mix, and heat through. Serve garnished with coriander leaves.

Spicy Szechuan Noodles

INGREDIENTS

Serves 4

350g/12oz thick noodles
175g/6oz cooked chicken,
   shredded
50g/2oz roasted cashew nuts

For the dressing

4 spring onions, chopped
30ml/2 tbsp chopped coriander
2 garlic cloves, chopped
30ml/2 tbsp smooth peanut butter
30ml/2 tbsp sweet chilli sauce
15ml/1 tbsp soy sauce
15ml/1 tbsp sherry vinegar
15ml/1 tbsp sesame oil
30ml/2 tbsp olive oil
30ml/2 tbsp chicken stock
   or water
10 toasted Szechuan peppercorns,
   ground

1 Cook the noodles in a saucepan of boiling water until just tender, following the directions on the packet. Drain, rinse under cold running water and drain well.

2 While the noodles are cooking combine all the ingredients for the dressing in a large bowl and whisk together well.

3 Add the noodles, shredded chicken and cashew nuts to the dressing, toss gently to coat and adjust the seasoning to taste. Serve at once.

COOK'S TIP

You could substitute cooked turkey or pork for the chicken for a change.

Sesame Noodles with Spring Onions

This simple but very tasty warm salad can be prepared and cooked in just a few minutes.

INGREDIENTS

Serves 4

2 garlic cloves, roughly chopped
30ml/2 tbsp Chinese sesame paste
15ml/1 tbsp dark sesame oil
30ml/2 tbsp soy sauce
30ml/2 tbsp rice wine
15ml/1 tbsp honey
pinch of five-spice powder
350g/12oz soba or
   buckwheat noodles
4 spring onions, finely
   sliced diagonally
50g/2oz beansprouts
7.5cm/3in piece of cucumber, cut
   into matchsticks
toasted sesame seeds
salt and freshly ground black pepper

1 Process the garlic, sesame paste, oil, soy sauce, rice wine, honey and five-spice powder with a pinch each of salt and pepper in a blender of food processor until smooth.

2 Cook the noodles in a saucepan of boiling water until just tender, following the directions on the packet. Drain the noodles immediately and tip them into a bowl.

3 Toss the hot noodles with the dressing and the spring onions. Top with the beansprouts, cucumber and sesame seeds and serve.

COOK'S TIP

If you can't find Chinese sesame paste, then use either tahini paste or smooth peanut butter instead.

Crispy Noodles with Mixed Vegetables

In this dish, rice vermicelli noodles are deep fried until crisp, then tossed into a colourful selection of stir-fried vegetables.

INGREDIENTS

Serves 4

2 large carrots
2 courgettes
4 spring onions
115g/4oz yard-long beans or
   green beans
115g/4oz dried vermicelli rice noodles
   or cellophane noodles
groundnut oil, for deep frying
2.5cm/1in fresh root ginger, shredded
1 fresh red chilli, sliced
115g/4oz fresh shiitake or button
   mushrooms, thickly sliced
few Chinese cabbage leaves,
   roughly shredded
75g/3oz beansprouts
30ml/2 tbsp light soy sauce
30ml/2 tbsp Chinese rice wine or
   dry sherry
5ml/1 tsp sugar
30ml/2 tbsp roughly torn fresh
   coriander leaves

COOK'S TIP

Vermicelli rice noodles, which are thin and brittle, look like a bundle of white hair. They cook almost instantly in hot liquid, provided they have first been soaked in warm water. Rice noodles can also be deep fried. Cellophane noodles, which are made from ground mung beans, look a little like bundles of candy floss. They are opaque white when dried and expand and become translucent after soaking. Cellophane noodles are also known as bean thread, transparent and glass noodles. Dried noodles must be soaked for 5 minutes in hot water before cooking.

---

1 Cut the carrots and courgettes into fine sticks. Shred the spring onions into similar-sized pieces. Trim the beans and cut them into short lengths.

2 Break the noodles into lengths of about 7.5cm/3in. Half-fill a wok with oil and heat it to 180°C/350°F. Deep fry the raw noodles, a handful at a time, for 1–2 minutes until puffed and crispy. Drain on kitchen paper. Pour off all but 30ml/2 tbsp of the oil.

3 Reheat the oil in the wok. When hot, add the beans and stir-fry for 2–3 minutes.

4 Add the ginger, red chilli, mushrooms, carrots and courgettes and stir-fry for 1–2 minutes. Add the Chinese cabbage, beansprouts and spring onions. Stir-fry for 1 minute, then add the soy sauce, rice wine or sherry and sugar. Cook, stirring, for about 30 seconds.

5 Add the noodles and coriander and toss to mix, taking care not to crush the noodles too much. Serve at once, piled up on a plate.

Plain Rice

Use long-grain or patna rice or fragrant rice from Thailand. Allow 50g/2oz raw rice per person. If you use fragrant Thai rice, omit the salt.

INGREDIENTS

Serves 4
225g/8oz/generous 1 cup rice
about 250ml/8fl oz/1 cup water
pinch of salt
2.5ml/½ tsp vegetable oil

1 Wash and rinse the rice. Place the rice in a saucepan and add the water. There should be no more than 2cm/¾in of water above the surface of the rice.

2 Bring to the boil, add the salt and oil, then stir to prevent the rice sticking to the bottom of the pan. Reduce the heat to very, very low, cover and cook for 15–20 minutes.

3 Remove from the heat and leave to stand, still covered, for 10 minutes. Fluff up the rice with a fork or spoon just before serving.

Egg-fried Rice

Use rice with a fairly firm texture. Ideally, the raw rice should be soaked in water for a short time before cooking.

INGREDIENTS

Serves 4
3 eggs
5ml/1 tsp salt
2 spring onions, finely chopped
30–45ml/2–3 tbsp vegetable oil
450g/1lb cooked rice
115g/4oz frozen peas

1 In a bowl, lightly beat the eggs with a pinch of the salt and a few pieces of the spring onions.

2 Heat the oil in a preheated wok, and lightly scramble the eggs.

3 Add the cooked rice and stir to make sure that each grain of rice is separated. Add the remaining salt, spring onions and the peas. Blend well, allow to heat through and serve.

Mango and Coconut Stir-fry

Choose a ripe mango for this recipe. If you buy one that is a little under-ripe, leave it in a warm place for a day or two before using.

INGREDIENTS

Serves 4
¼ coconut
1 large, ripe mango
juice of 2 limes
rind of 2 limes, finely grated
15ml/1 tbsp sunflower oil
15g/½ oz butter
30ml/2 tbsp clear honey
crème fraîche, to serve

1 Prepare the coconut flakes by draining the milk from the coconut and peeling the flesh with a vegetable peeler.

2 Peel the mango. Cut the stone out of the middle of the fruit. Cut each half of the mango into slices.

3 Place the mango slices in a bowl and pour over the lime juice and rind, to marinate them.

4 Meanwhile heat a wok, then add 10ml/2 tsp of the oil. When the oil is hot, add the butter. When the butter has melted, stir in the coconut flakes and stir-fry for 1–2 minutes until the coconut is golden brown. Remove and drain on kitchen paper. Wipe out the wok. Strain the mango slices, reserving the juice.

5 Heat the wok and add the remaining oil. When the oil is hot, add the mango and stir-fry for 1–2 minutes, then add the juice and allow to bubble and reduce for 1 minute. Stir in the honey, sprinkle on the coconut flakes and serve with crème fraîche.

--- COOK'S TIP ---

You can sometimes buy "fresh" coconut that has already been cracked open and is sold in pieces ready for use from supermarkets, but buying the whole nut ensures greater freshness. Choose one that is heavy for its size and shake it so that you can hear the milk sloshing about. A "dry" coconut will almost certainly have rancid flesh. You can simply crack the shell with a hammer, preferably with the nut inside a plastic bag, but it may be better to pierce the two ends with a sharp nail or skewer first in order to collect and save the coconut milk. An alternative method is to drain the milk first and then heat the nut briefly in the oven until it cracks. Whichever method you choose, it is then fairly easy to extract the flesh and chop or shave it.

Wonton Twists

These little twists are perfect when you want a quick snack.

INGREDIENTS

Makes 24
12 wonton wrappers
oil for deep frying
1 egg, beaten
15ml/1 tbsp black sesame seeds
icing sugar for dusting (optional)

1 Cut the wonton wrappers in half and make a lengthways slit in the centre of each piece with a sharp knife.

----- COOK'S TIP -----

Use ordinary sesame seeds in place of the black ones if you prefer.

2 Take one wonton at a time and pull one end through the slit, stretching it a little as you go.

3 Heat the oil in a deep fryer or large saucepan to 190°C/375°F. Meanwhile brush each twist with a little beaten egg.

4 Dip the wonton twists briefly in the sesame seeds to coat them lightly, then add a few twists at a time to the oil – do not overcrowd the pan. Fry for 1–2 minutes on each side until crisp and light golden brown. Remove each twist and drain on kitchen paper. Dust the wonton twists with icing sugar, if you like, and serve at once.

Fried Wontons and Ice Cream

Americans have their cookies and ice cream – here is the Chinese equivalent. Serve it with fresh or poached fruits or fruit sauces for an impressive treat.

INGREDIENTS

Serves 4
oil for deep frying
12 wonton wrappers
8 scoops of your favourite
  ice cream

----- COOK'S TIP -----

Try using two flavours of ice cream – chocolate and strawberry perhaps, or vanilla and coffee. For a sophisticated adults-only treat, drizzle over a spoonful of your favourite liqueur.

1 Heat the oil in a deep fryer or large saucepan to 190°C/375°F.

3 Leave the cooked wontons to drain on kitchen paper.

2 Add a few wonton wrappers at a time so that they do not crowd the pan too much. Fry for 1–2 minutes on each side until the wrappers are crisp and light golden brown.

4 To serve, place one wonton on each plate. Place a scoop of ice cream on top of each wonton. Top with a second wonton, then add another ball of ice cream and finish with a final wonton. Serve at once.

INDEX